BOSS Business Launch Planner

Step-By-Step Guide To Earning Income Leveraging Skills, Knowledge, and Expertise You Already Have

ALL RIGHTS RESERVED. This publication contains copyrighted content. The content contained herein cannot be distributed, revised, or otherwise used without my express written consent.

AFFILIATE DISCLAIMER. Some of the links in this publication are affiliate links which means that I earn money if you choose to purchase that service. Please know I do not choose which products and services to promote based upon which pay me the most, I only recommend products and/or services from reputable companies. You will never pay more for an item when using my affiliate link. In fact, you may pay less since I negotiate special offers for my readers that are not available elsewhere.

DISCLAIMER AND/OR LEGAL NOTICES: The information presented herein represents my professional views as of the date of publication. Because of the rate with which conditions change, this author reserves the right to alter and update her opinion based on the new conditions. This publication is for informational purposes only. While every attempt has been made to verify the information provided in this publication, neither the author nor her affiliates/ partners assume any responsibility for errors, inaccuracies, or omissions. Any slights of people or organizations are unintentional. If advice concerning legal or related matters is needed, the services of a fully qualified professional should be sought. This publication is not intended for use as a source of legal or accounting advice. You should be aware of any laws which govern business transactions or other business practices in your country and state. Any reference to any person or business whether living or dead is purely coincidental.
Copyright ©

Time To Launch That Business You Have Been Dreaming About…

Congratulations on deciding to start your business!

If this is the first time you are meeting me, my name is Michele Davis. I am a Business Coach and the host of Da Boss Experience Podcast.

Before I get into what you can expect from this business launch planner, I want to share a little bit about my entrepreneurial journey and why I decided to create this planner in the first place.

I landed in the world of entrepreneurship back in 2016 at the age of 45. I just left an organization that sucked all of my passion for nonprofit services right out of my body. Of course, my initial response was to just change jobs. Then after sending out literally a hundred or more resumes and getting few interviews and no job offers, I quickly admitted to myself that it was time to look at alternative sources of income.

As I contemplated what was next for me, I decided to start a business. My initial urge to be my own boss came from the frustration of not being able to find a job. Then I realized I had spent 20+ years repressing all my creativity and ideas to carry out the vision of someone else. Why not spend the next 20 years focusing on my needs, goals, desires, and dreams.

I had no idea how to launch a business, I did not personally know any entrepreneurs, nor was I aware of any business owners in my family at the time. I just knew I needed more control over my time and income.

So I decided to turn to social media and YouTube to find a resource to figure out the type of business to launch. I had no idea what I wanted to sell and did not feel like I had any obvious skills or talents to monetize. So I decided to find a business coach to help me fast track my business success.

While I ended up working with a few coaches at the beginning stages of starting my business, I experienced a lot of frustration just trying to get my business started. I think the main problem I had with the coaches I worked with back in 2016 is they did not know how to create a starting point for me. By starting point, I mean a simple process that involved aligning me with a business model based on what I already knew and enjoyed doing.

They only wanted to steer me toward trends or the models they said were profitable. The problem with trends is they do not last. The other issue with this practice is just because something is profitable for someone else, does not mean you will find that same success even if you duplicated the same business model.

Just because someone wants to start a business does not mean they are a clean slate. When you get to a certain age, you have an abundance of life and career experience that can be monetized as a successful service-based business. You just need a coach that believes in you and is capable of packaging up what you already know into a program, product, or service.

That is why I am committed to utilizing my podcast, digital products, and coaching services to give other late-blooming entrepreneurs like me the tools and support to fearlessly transition from a career they no longer feel passionate about to starting their own business.

What You Can Expect From This Planner

So many new entrepreneurs struggle with figuring out where to start, what to sell, and how to sell it when it comes to launching a business.

It is not uncommon for people to spend months or even years downloading eBooks, watching webinars, and buying programs, only to realize they are still stuck when it comes to getting their business idea off the ground.

While it seems like there are tons of resources available online to help you start a business, few offer an A-to-Z approach. In fact, most of these resources often leave out vital information that prevents you from even moving forward to get your business started. So you find yourself sort of back at ground zero because you have the information, but no strategy or tool to implement what you have learned. This Business Launch Blueprint Planner takes care of that problem.

Inside this planner, I share my Business Launch Blueprint to help you:

Bonus: Set Your Goals

Bonus: Prepare Your Mindset for Entrepreneurship

Step 1: Determine What You Already Know and Love Doing

Step 2: Define Your Business Idea

Step 3: Develop Your Business Plan

Step 4: Launch Your Business

Step 5: Create Sustainable Business Systems

This Business Launch Planner is not a notebook where you jot down a bunch of great ideas and nothing happens after that. Treat this planner like a reference that you will refer back to repeatedly as you get your business launched. **Now let's start planning your business!**

Table of Contents

Set Your Goals	8
Prepare Your Mindset for Entrepreneurship	15
Step 1 - Determine What You Already Know and Love Doing	20
Step 2 - Define Your Business Idea	24
Step 3 - Develop Your Business Plan	28
Step 4 - Launch Your Business	48
Step 5 - Create Sustainable Business Systems	81
Next Steps	88

Set Your Goals

Why Set Goals

Anytime you start something new, you are guaranteed to have a bunch of thoughts and ideas rolling around in your head. Setting goals enables you to not only know what you ultimately want to achieve, but a clear direction to be successful in your endeavor.

Starting A Business Is Not A Standalone Event I am giving you a fair warning that starting a business is a rollercoaster. While goal setting makes things easier, it does not eliminate the craziness that naturally comes with entrepreneurship. You will have good days, but you will have some frustrating and stressful days, particularly as you work to get your business off the ground and profitable.

As you set your goals, be mindful that starting a business is not a standalone venture. Your progress or lack thereof to get your business started is impacted by other responsibilities and events in your life. Starting a business may take you away from time with your family and friends. So it is important to assess and be honest about where you are right now so you can set realistic goals that you can accomplish.

Here Is My Strategy for Setting Effective Goals

In this section, you will answer some questions about your goals. So It is important to think about what it is you want and why you want it.

As you set your goals, you want to make sure your goals are…

Specific. Goals are easier to accomplish when you specify what you want to achieve. For example, saying that you want to start a business is vague. You will need to be clear on specifically the type of business you are starting to plan and set your goals accordingly. At this stage, you may or may not know exactly the type of business you want to start and that is ok. By the end of this planner, you will be able to define your goals with specificity. That is when you want to come back to this section and update your goals as needed.

Measurable. Setting a measurable goal is simply quantifying what you plan to accomplish. For example, you can set a goal to enroll 5 clients per month in your coaching service. It will be clear each month whether you met your goal because what you want to achieve can be measured.

Achievable. To make a goal achievable it must be something that can be accomplished within the period you establish. For example, it is unrealistic to set a goal that you will start a business over the weekend. You may be able to make progress toward the "Big Goal" of starting a business, but to launch a business with a foundation and infrastructure for success is not achievable in such a short timeframe. So you have to ask yourself if your goal and timeframe are achievable considering all of your commitments (job, kids, spouse, etc…).

Realistic. You want to set big goals. However, both your expectations and goals need to match your time, resources, and abilities. For example, if you are already working 40 hours a week at a full-time job, it may be unrealistic to set a goal to work 40 hours per week on your business. Instead, think about what you need to accomplish each day, week, and month and set your goals accordingly.

Time-Bound. Your goals need a target date of completion. Target dates help you move forward to your next set of priorities. Without firm deadlines for your goals, you end up on the path of the forever project that never actually gets completed.

As you start to set new goals, don't hesitate to let go of old goals. Your new goals are a better fit for where you are headed with the launch and eventually the growth of your business. Review your goals as you progress and make room for changing priorities.

Now It Is Time For You To Set Your First Goals

I want you to set your first goal based on what you want to accomplish with this Business Launch Planner. Now obviously you want direction to start your business, but what else do you want to achieve? In other words, what do YOU WANT to walk away with when you finish the last page of this planner? Stay focused on what You Want instead of what you DO NOT want. Write your thoughts below.

_____

_____

_____

Now that you know what you want to get from this Business Launch Planner, use the lines below to express how accomplishing this goal (s) changes your life, family, and finances?

_____

_____

_____

NOW CLAIM YOUR GOAL BY STATING!

" I _____ claim the goal of achieving

_____ by blank _____, 20____ "

Print this statement and post it somewhere visible to you. Reflect on it every day, so your goal stays fresh on your mind.

Erase Those Limiting Beliefs

Now Let's Tackle Your Limiting Beliefs...When you wrote your goal, what negative thought popped into your mind about your ability to accomplish it? Write down everything that came to mind here.

_____

_____

_____

Just like limiting beliefs can jeopardize your ability to achieve your goals, so can distractions. So think about everything going on in your life. What are your biggest distractions right now that can hinder your goal of starting a business? List them and commit to **NOT** allowing your distractions to prevent you from completing this Business Launch Planner and starting your business.

_____

_____

_____

Remember you don't want to take time to complete this planner only for nothing to happen afterward. Commit now to let go of any limiting beliefs and distractions that can prevent you from staying focused and on track to start your business. **Now, let's work on your mindset!**

Prepare Your Mindset For Entrepreneurship

Why Preparing Your Mindset Is Important

Part of you is excited at the thought of being a business owner. However, the other part of you is questioning whether you have expertise that qualifies you to get paid to help someone else solve a problem or achieve a transformation.

Preparing your mindset for entrepreneurship is about having confidence that you possess a skill, expert knowledge, or have an experience you can package up into a paid program, product, or service.

As you work through this **Business Launch Planner** and begin to document your ideas, you are going to force yourself to…

- Establish Big Goals that will scare you to the point of questioning your ability to achieve that level of success
- Think about having the success that you never thought was possible
- Challenge beliefs around money and wealth that block you from achieving success

So as you move through this **section**, be clear on what success means to you. Be honest about any fears you have about your ability to have success in life. Believe in yourself enough to know you deserve success.

Steer Clear Of Negative Thinking

Negative words and phrases are neither motivating nor conducive to success. As you start the process of shifting your mindset, you also need to permanently remove negative words and phrases from your vocabulary.

Here's an example of some negative words and phrases you want to steer clear of:

"I can't do this!"

"I'm not smart enough!"

"People like me can't do stuff like that!"

...And any other negative thoughts that pop into your head.

What you focus on expands. That is why you have to constantly tell yourself "I CAN DO THIS" and other positive affirmations.

So now I want you to answer a few questions...

What is the reason behind your commitment to put in the hard work necessary to start your business?

_____

_____

_____

Write down 3 things you can do daily to stay motivated to get things done (ex. place affirmations around your home and office, create a schedule to stay on track, establish daily goals).

_____

_____

_____

What kept you from starting a business in the past?

_____

_____

_____

How will you deal with the obstacles you will undoubtedly face starting your business (ex. time, money constraints)?

_____

_____

_____

How would your life change if you were doing work that made you happy? Write out your vision of what your best life looks like. Refer back to this page when you need the motivation to keep going when things are rough and seem stagnant.

_____

_____

_____

_____

_____

_____

_____

_____

Step 1
Determine What You Already Know and Love Doing

Start Your Entrepreneurship Journey By Determining What You Already Know and Love Doing

Some people will tell you passion has nothing to do with starting a business. There are a few problems with this advice. The first problem is just because a certain type of business is successful for one person, does not mean that you will experience the same results.

The second problem with this advice is you do not want to spend time and money getting a business started that you do not feel interested in or passionate about. Eventually, you will feel like you just created another job you hate.

The third problem with this advice is it is hard to engage authentically with potential clients if you have no connection to what you sell. If you start a business solely based on what you think is profitable in an industry you know nothing about, it will not be long before potential clients recognize they are more passionate about what you sell than you are.

Aside from the other problems I mentioned, why would you want to disregard what makes you happy when it comes to starting your own business.

Your passions, skills, and expertise are a starting point to launching a business you love. While becoming your own boss is exciting, it can also be challenging when things do not go as planned. You will find it hard to weather the storm through rough times if you do not enjoy what you do.

So let us explore and identify your superpowers...a.k.a what you're passionate about and what you're good at.

Define Your Strengths

Using the prompts below, describe your passions, interests, experiences, and skills. Do not worry about editing right now. Write down everything that comes to mind.

What are you most passionate about? What is it you love to do?

_____

_____

_____

What are you good at? Is there something people are constantly asking you to help them with?

_____

_____

_____

What are your experiences? What have you overcome that could enable you to help someone else experience the same transformation? Do a brain dump of everything that comes to mind.

_____

_____

_____

_____

_____

_____

_____

_____

Step 2

Define Your Business Idea

Establish A Business Idea

Now that you have outlined your goals, prepared your mindset for entrepreneurship, identified your passions and interests, it's time to define your business idea.

Review your responses to the questions in Step 1 and use this section to link each experience, skill, or circumstance you have overcome to a specific problem you can solve. Once again, this is a brain dump so write down all of your thoughts.

_____

_____

_____

_____

_____

_____

_____

_____

Now, look at your list from the previous page. Using the space below, write the things you are passionate about or the problems you could envision yourself solving for people below.

_____

_____

_____

_____

_____

_____

_____

_____

Now jot down what service (s) you can offer to solve each problem based on your skills, knowledge, and expertise.

_____

_____

_____

_____

_____

_____

_____

_____

Step 3

Develop Your Business Plan

Examine Your Market

So now that you have some business ideas on paper, use this section to conduct market research to ensure there is profit potential for the product or service you identified in Step 2.

How many monthly internet searches are made related to the problem you solve? Use free resources online like Google Search, Google Trends, Ubersuggest, Google Keyword Planner, and Answer the Public to see whether people are searching to solve the problem you want to solve for people.

_____

_____

_____

What trends are happening in your desired industry right now that you could take advantage of in your business?

_____

_____

_____

_____

Who are your competitors? Make note of their price and product offerings.

_____

_____

_____

How do you plan to position your product or service in the market to compete with the other businesses already providing the same service? For example, look at your market to detect if there is a need not being met by the competition or a group of people not targeted.

_____

_____

_____

Define Your Target Audience

You cannot sell your product or service to everyone with a pulse. There is a core group of people who resonate deeply with you, your brand, and what you offer. This core group is your target audience. So you need to define who those people are.

Knowing your target audience is the key to finding the "right people" online. Once you locate your target audience you can learn more about what they need, their pain points, where they are hanging out, who influences them, and so on. Having this information allows you to create content and engage in marketing activities that attract your target audience.

Once you know who your target audience is then it is time to drill deeper into how to find your dream customer or ideal client (the person that will ultimately buy your program, product, or service).

Finding Your Target Audience Online

The thing you have to remember is your target audience is already online. With so much happening online, it can feel overwhelming trying to navigate every possible online platform just to find your target audience.

So instead of thinking about spreading yourself across multiple platforms to find your target, focus on the problem you solve and who best benefits from that solution. Then you want to think about a public figure, influencer, or other high-profile people that already engage with the same people that will benefit from your program, product, or service. As you identify these people, list their names on a spreadsheet.

Document everywhere these public figures, influencers, or other high-profile people show up online and offline using your spreadsheet. This could be a Facebook group, LinkedIn group, Instagram, or even an offline event. Once you know who these people are and where they are engaging with their audience (a.k.a…the same audience you want to work with), join these groups and attend these events.

This is where market research comes in handy.

Once you are connected to the various online and offline groups, pay attention to the needs of that audience. Listen out for questions they ask and problems they discuss. This information helps you develop a program, product, or service that helps your target audience solve a Big Problem.

Now that you know a little more about your target audience, let's define your ideal client using my client avatar template.

Create Your Ideal Client Avatar

Your target audience is a general group of people your program, product, or service benefits. However, your Ideal Client (also known as your Dream Customer) is a refined version of your target audience. Your Ideal Client is the exact person your program, product, or service is designed to help.

When you create an Ideal Client Avatar, you outline a hypothetical profile of your potential buyer. It is going to feel really weird creating this fictitious person. Just keep in mind this profile allows you to understand your Ideal Client on a deeper level.

Use the prompts on the next few pages to create your Ideal Client Avatar.

Ideal Client Avatar Name _____

Make Your Ideal Client Avatar Real

Use magazines or the internet to find an image that represents the image of your ideal client avatar.

Define the demographics for your Ideal Client (ex. age, gender, marital status, education, location of residence, career, income, single mom). Your description needs to be based on the market research you performed earlier in this Boss Business Launch Planner.

_____

_____

_____

Identify the pain points your Ideal Client is experiencing. Be sure you focus on the pain points they are willing to pay money for to get a solution to their problem.

_____

_____

_____

What is the desired result your Ideal Client wants? Do they believe your program, product, or service will give them the solution they want?

_____

_____

_____

What other programs, products, and services have they tried? What is the reason they were not successful before?

_____

_____

_____

Where do they spend their time online? Include specific social media platforms, Facebook Groups, and other forums.

_____

_____

_____

What influencers are they following on social media and YouTube? Note what the influencers are known for as well.

_____

_____

_____

What are their hobbies and interests?

_____

_____

_____

What do they read (i.e., books, magazines) and watch (i.e., tv)?

_____

_____

_____

What type of podcasts do they listen to?

_____

_____

_____

So why is all of this information important to know about your Ideal Client?

Based on my experience as a Business Coach, I can tell why so many new and not so new entrepreneurs struggle to get clients. Most entrepreneurs do not take the time to do what you just did, which is think about what problem they solve, who they solve the problem for, what matters to that Ideal Client, and what factors into their buying decision. Once you know these things about your Ideal Client, creating content and attracting them to you online becomes easier.

Because you took the time to complete this BOSS Business Launch Planner, you are already steps ahead of so many other entrepreneurs.

So whenever you sit down to create content or engage in any marketing activity whatsoever, all you have to do is think about the needs, pain points, and interests of your Ideal Client Avatar. Then create content that addresses their pain points and positions you as the expert they need to solve their problem.

Now That You Know Who You Serve, It Is Time To Create Your Offer

Entrepreneurs often mistake their program, product, or service as an offer. These things are merely a tool to help you solve a Big Problem or deliver a Transformation to your clients.

So imagine when your clients first contact you for assistance. They are sad or dissatisfied with their current situation. So they are looking to you for a solution that is going to make them happy. Your offer is a clearly defined process that takes them from a place of sadness to happiness.

For example, let us say I am a health coach offering fitness and food plans for my clients. There is nothing unique about these services because potential clients can buy health and food plans from any health coach. These fitness and food plans are just tools a health coach would use in their business.

An offer linked to a specific outcome is more appealing than just a basic service. So if you are a health coach with a 5 step process to help your client lose 10 pounds in 30-days, this is an offer.

The more refined your offer is, the more attractive it is to your Ideal Client.

That is why it is so important to understand the needs of your Ideal Client, who is influencing them, and what makes them go from observer to buyer.

So in this section, think about your step-by-step process for delivering results to your client. The more details you provide for prospective clients upfront, the likelihood increases that they qualify themselves as a candidate for your program, product, or service.

Package Your Offer

Now it's time to think about how you will package your service into an offer. The offer you create needs to be developed in a way that's both appealing and solves a Big Problem for your Ideal Client. Use this section to structure your service by detailing exactly what a client receives to take them from a place of despair or unhappiness to their happy place (transformation/joy).

While it may be tempting to solve several problems for your ideal client, your offer needs to focus on solving one Big Problem for them.

Otherwise, you'll end up with two issues. The first issue is you'll create an offer that ends up being confusing for your ideal client to understand because you are trying to solve too many problems. The second problem is you may not end up solving your client's problem at all because you are focusing on too many problems at the same time.

So now it is time to lay everything out in a framework…

What is your "Big Promise" to your clients? In other words, what is the outcome your client receives as a result of working with you? Remember, you should have identified your Big Promise in the previous section.

_____

_____

_____

Explain how you plan to get your clients to the outcome they are seeking in 5 to 7 steps. If you offer a service like graphic design or virtual assistant, then use this section to outline your service packages and/or categories below.

_____

_____

_____

Take each of the steps you just identified and list details. In other words, define what is included in each step or package level.

_____

_____

_____

Now think about how you want to deliver the service. Do you want to use your skills and knowledge to complete the work yourself, coach someone through a problem, or do you want to be more of an advisor that guides or teaches others how to do something? Outline delivery details below.

_____

_____

_____

How will you deliver your offer (ex. Zoom co-working sessions, prerecorded course, audio calls, Live training, done-for-you service, Voxer)?

_____

_____

_____

What will your client need to provide on their end to enable you to complete the service?

_____

_____

_____

How long will you work with each client (ex. 30 days, 90 days, etc.)? If you plan to offer a done-for-you service, what is the turnaround time for you to complete the service?

_____

_____

_____

How many clients will you work with at one time? This depends on what your offer entails, and how much work you need to perform on your end.

_____

_____

_____

Write Your Promise Statement

Now write a promise statement that defines who you help (target audience), what you help them to achieve (outcome), and how you help them achieve it (big promise).

Here are a couple of examples...

"I help postpartum women return to their prepregnancy weight without starving themselves or engaging in time-intensive workouts."

"I help homeschooling moms develop their child's unique learning journey while working full-time."

Now write your promise statement below.

_____

_____

Price Your Offer

When it comes to pricing your programs, products, and services, you want to:

- Create an offer that is attractive to your Ideal Client
- Set your offer price according to the overall value of your program, product, or service
- Base your price on the overall project and outcome
- Establish tiered priced packages when appropriate

Use this section to map out tentative base pricing for your program, product, or service.

_____

_____

_____

How Will You Operate

So now that you have some business ideas on paper, use this section to plan out the foundational aspect of your business.

What is your planned legal setup (ex. LLC, S-Corp)? Read my Blog Post (https://bit.ly/LLCblogpost) to learn if an LLC is right for you.

_____

Create a budget identifying your anticipated costs for launch, marketing, product creation, tools, packaging, shipping, delivery, trademarks, business related subscriptions, website hosting, and start-up, or other business costs.

_____

_____

_____

How do you plan to fund your business expenses?

_____

_____

_____

Do you need a third party to produce any aspect of your program, product, or service? If so, who are your vendors or partners?

_____

_____

_____

Describe your client onboarding process. Include the names of forms you will use as well.

_____

_____

_____

What challenges or barriers to entry do you anticipate in regards to supplying, marketing, selling, and managing your program, product, or service?

_____

_____

_____

State your monthly and annual revenue goals.

_____

_____

_____

Depending on the details of your business, you may need an Employer Identification Number (EIN) to pay federal taxes, hire employees, open a bank account, and apply for business licenses and permits. An EIN is your federal tax ID. It's free to apply for an EIN. Write your EIN number below or not applicable if you plan to use your social security number for business.

_____

_____

_____

Step 4

Launch Your Business

Prepare Your Business for Launch

The online world is a cesspool of unscrupulous people. It is not uncommon to hear about someone hiring a service provider they met online that ultimately did not perform the work they paid for or produced a poor quality result. So people are skeptical when making service related purchases online.

People want to know they are doing business with a credible, professional person and/or a company that is going to perform the work they are signing on to receive. So you have to show up online as a professional coach, consultant, or other service provider that is invested in your business. This means you need to invest some time and some money to create a professional visual identity for your business before you accept your first client.

Use this section as a checklist to establish a business identity that builds the trust you need with prospective clients right from the start.

Securing A Business Name For Use Online and Offline. The first step to establishing a business identity is choosing a business name. Whatever business name you select, you want to make sure you can secure the name as a domain name for your website and on social media. Securing your business name across available platforms makes it harder for another business to mistakenly or intentionally use the same name you are using for their business.

Once you brainstorm a few names, you need to take some additional action before finalizing your business name. First, you want to check domain availability. You can use dadigitaldiva.com, or any other reputable domain name provider to purchase your new domain name.

Next, you want to make sure the name is not trademarked or in use by another business. So visit uspto.gov to check the trademark status of a business name. I also suggest you conduct a Google search for the name as well.

Then make sure your desired business name is available on the major social media platforms (Facebook, Instagram, and Twitter) even if you do not plan to use a particular platform.

Your domain name and social media usernames need to have the same spelling (including symbols, letter casing) for consistency. Otherwise, your potential clients will have trouble finding you.

Once you confirm the name is available as a domain name and on the major social media platforms, you can finalize your domain name purchase at dadigitaldiva.com or any other reputable domain name provider. Domain names are typically nonrefundable no matter where you purchase them so be absolutely sure you selected the best domain name for your business and double-check the spelling before finalizing your domain name purchase. **Please note the only way to legally protect your business name from use by another individual or company is through a trademark.**

Record your business details in this section:

Business Name.

_____

Domain Name.

_____

Social Media Usernames and Platforms.

_____

Professional Logo. Logos allow your business and brand to have a professional, distinctive, identifiable look. While there are websites that offer a DIY logo design option, these designs are often only available as a low resolution image. Use websites like Fiverr (fiverr.com) and Upwork (upwork.com) to find a graphic designer to create a high resolution logo and favicon for use on your website and marketing materials.

Write the designer/website name you will use to create your logo below:

_____

Professional Email Address. Once you have a domain name, I recommend you steer clear of using a Gmail or any other free account to conduct your business. When you take the necessary steps to establish yourself as a business, your customers take note that you are a professional that is here to stay and not someone that is looking to temporarily set up shop. Using the same name you use for your domain name, purchase a professional email address with companies like Da Digital Diva (dadigitaldiva.com) and Google Workspace (workspace.google.com).

Write your new email address below:

_____

Website. Websites allow you to have a hub for potential clients to learn more about you and your business and make purchases. Whether they find a business owner online or offline, potential clients feel more at ease making a buying decision when they can find a professional company website with information about the business owner and the company.

Create a website that is visually appealing, easy to navigate, and displays basic information about your business such as your services, frequently asked questions, your story about why you started your business, and contact information. This can even be a one-page website.

You can hire a website designer on Upwork (upwork.com) or build your own with templates available on Da Digital Diva (dadigitaldiva.com), Wix (wix.com), Squarespace (squarespace.com), or any other reputable website company. Keep in mind even though some companies advertise free websites, there are limitations for branding the website with your own domain. So be sure to read what is included before you finalize your purchase.

As a reminder, your website name is the same as your domain name. Write the name of the website company you plan to use below:

_____

Font. It is important to be consistent with branding in your business. When potential clients are faced with a purchasing decision, you want to avoid anything that appears distracting to the individual viewing your website, social media pages, or marketing materials. Select no more than 3 font types to use for all written and online materials and content. Websites like Google Fonts (fonts.google.com) can help you select fonts for your business.

Write the name of the fonts you selected for easy reference:

_____

Brand Color Palette. Colors produce feelings and emotion in people, so you want to be mindful of this when selecting colors for your business. Select colors that evoke the feeling you want for your brand and business. For example, if you are planning on being a grief coach, you may want to steer clear of colors that may be disruptive (ex. Black) to someone seeking your services. Select 3-5 brand colors based on what you want your clients to feel when they encounter your business. Be consistent with the same colors everywhere you show up online and offline. Use websites like Coolors (coolors.co) and Adobe (color.adobe.com/create/color-wheel) to help you choose your brand color palette.

Write the hex code and RGB or CYAN codes for your selected colors below:

_____

Payment Processor (ex. PayPal, Stripe) . Before you accept your first client, you need a system to process client payments. You can choose to invoice your client or automate the payment process using services like PayPal (paypal.com), Square (square.com), or Stripe (stripe.com). Once you select a payment processor, display the electronic payment options on your website.

Write your payment processor company name below:

_____

Address. You never want potential clients to feel like you are hiding your location or that you are pretending to be in one country and you are actually based in another country. Most people want to know where a company is located before making a decision to do business. Where a business is based matters in the event of returns, refunds, disputes, time zone considerations, among other things.

You do not want to use your home address on your website. However, if you are in the U.S., you can open a P.O. Box or purchase a virtual address with a company like iPostal1 (ipostal1.com) to legitimize your business. Be sure to include your business address on your website, in your email communications with prospective clients, and on your marketing materials.

Write your business address and service provider name below:

_____

Phone Number. If you plan to engage with clients by telephone, you may not want to use your personal cell phone or home number. You can get a Google Voice (voice.google.com) number free of charge. The downside to Google Voice is that the callers know that you are using a free service to mask your real number. The alternative to Google Voice is companies like Freedom Voice (freedomvoice.com) or Grasshopper (grasshopper.com) that enable you to set up a business number with a unique greeting that rings right into your mobile phone. Once you have a business number, Include your business phone number in full view on your website, business email communications, and on your marketing materials.

Write your business phone number and service provider name below:

_____

Client Agreement. Client agreements are essential for service-based businesses owners. Your client agreement defines the exact service you plan to perform, the cost of the service, expectations you have of your client, refund process, and exit clauses so you can leave the agreement in the event it is no longer beneficial to continue working together. While it may seem like a client agreement is overkill, having the terms of your services clearly defined is a lifesaver in the event of a client dispute.

You can get a basic client agreement from companies like Honeybook (honeybook.com) and Rocket Lawyer (rocketlawyer.com). While these companies provide general agreements, the documents may not account for certain laws in your state.

That is why I always recommend my clients pay the small monthly fee to use services like LegalShield (bit.ly/business-launch-resource) to get advice from an actual attorney in the event of a dispute. LegalShield connects you with a local attorney in your area that can review your client agreement and recommend terms and clauses that provide additional protections in accordance with the laws in your state.

Outline how you plan to create and/or acquire a client service agreement for your business.

_____

_____

_____

Now that you have established your business identity and you have a business agreement, it is time to discuss the marketing plan to launch your business.

Launching Your Business

When you introduce your business to the world it should not feel like you just woke up one day and decided to start a business. There is marketing work to be done in the months and/or weeks leading up to you selling your first product or service.

The key to making steady sales in your business is to develop a marketing plan that includes a strategy to attract people that have never heard of you or your brand. Marketing plans are not a one-size-fits-all approach. You want to test different strategies to determine what gets you the best results for your business.

While I outline many marketing activities in this section, this is not an exhaustive list of all of the possible marketing strategies you can incorporate in your business. So use these activities to develop a plan specifically designed for your audience, budget, time, resources, and business.

Some of the activities I mention in this section are short-term strategies to get clients into your business quickly. I also outline several other strategies for you to consider implementing as a part of your long-term business marketing plan.

Now let us get started on your marketing plan!

Business Marketing Ideas

Social Media. Once you know the platform where your target audience hangs out, social media is a very effective tool to market your business. Social media is not a magic wand when it comes to getting clients. You have to be consistent on the platform, create content that attracts your target audience, and build an audience of people that are similar to your ideal client.

It is also important to know that not every platform will yield the same results for you. Some platforms reward you for using video, while other platforms will push you into paid ads just to get your business noticed.

Answer the questions below to gain clarity on how you will use social media to launch your new business.

What social media platform will you use on a consistent basis? Make sure you confirmed this social media platform is where your target audience hangs out and write the name below.

_____

What are the 3 to 4 core topic areas you will focus on related to the problem you solve?

_____

What is the frequency you will post or go Live on the platform? Be realistic and think about how often you can show up to post or go Live.

_____

Identify 14 posts ideas stemming from the 3 to 4 core topics you selected. Write out your ideas here or in the form of a content calendar so you can ensure what you create reflects what you want to deliver to your target audience.

_____

_____

_____

_____

_____

_____

_____

_____

Paid Advertising (Facebook, Instagram, Google, YouTube). Paid advertising is probably the quickest way to bring attention to your new business. However, paid advertising is not economically friendly particularly when you are just starting your business. So, if you plan to use paid advertising, seek assistance from an expert to help you develop an effective advertising campaign.

In the meantime, answer the questions below to determine if paid advertising is right for your business launch.

What is your budget for paid advertising?

_____

Do you have money to hire an agency, coach, or to purchase a course to learn about advertising? If yes, how much?

_____

If you are running paid ads to launch your business, what platform will you use for your advertising campaign?

_____

Are you prepared to lose money to test different advertising strategies and campaigns?

_____

Influencer Marketing. Influencer marketing is a short-term strategy to get your business in front of your target audience pretty quickly. This type of marketing involves you paying someone to share your program, product, or service with their social media audience.

Just like with paid advertising, you have to have a budget and strategy for influencer marketing. You also must choose an influencer (s) with a highly engaged social media following of people that you desire to serve.

Influencer marketing can be tricky because you may not get the outcome or sales from a single influencer ad. On the bright side, influencer marketing could still be effective and is typically cheaper than paying for social media and other paid advertising.

Do you have a budget for influencer marketing?

_____

Remember the spreadsheet you created previously containing the names of public figures, influencers, and other high-profile people already serving your target audience? List the names of influencers below that offer promotional opportunities. Be sure to also record below the cost and the terms of the promotion (ex. length of the promotion, story vs. feed, personal testimony vs. post).

_____

_____

_____

_____

_____

_____

_____

_____

_____

_____

Tap Into Your Network. Tapping into your network simply means notifying everyone you know that you are starting a business and need their support. You want to contact your network in a personal and authentic way. Your network is basically anyone you have a connection with personally or professionally.

Write out a quick blurb (150 - 250 characters) about your business to help you convey to your network what your business is about. Also be sure to include in your communication what it means to support your business (ex. sharing your post, purchasing from you, sending an email to their network) so your network knows how they can help you.

Write the names/groups of a minimum of 25 people you will notify about your business launch. Include telephone numbers so you easily contact them.

_____

_____

_____

_____

_____

_____

Email Marketing. Having an email list means you have a captive group of people already interested in your business that you can regularly email to market your sales and other promotions. While building an email list is a long-term marketing strategy, you need to lay the foundation for email marketing right from the launch of your business.

By collecting email addresses from people that are interested in your business right from the start you build a list of potential buyers that may purchase from you at a future date. So as you implement your short-term business launch activities, think about how you can collect an email address from people as they show interest in your new business.

Email marketing requires you to set goals and develop a strategy to guide your actions. While this Business Launch Planner cannot possibly teach you email marketing, you definitely want to commit to learning this important strategy. Answer the prompts below to determine the role email marketing will play in your long-term marketing plan.

When will you ask a potential client for their email address? Think about if you will have a popup on your website, give them something for free in exchange for their email, or use some other strategy to get email subscribers.

_____

How often will you send email content to your subscribers?

_____

Write 5 email topics you can send to your future subscribers based on the pain points you previously identified.

_____

_____

_____

_____

_____

Webinar. A webinar (sometimes referred to as Masterclass) is a presentation style mini-training that offers your target audience a solution to one of their pain points. The goal of the webinar is to provide enough information so attendees trust you enough to buy your program, product, or service as the solution to their problem.

A webinar is most effective Live, but can also be pre-recorded. Webinars are also a great client acquisition tool if you have a strategy to get enough attendees to make it worth your time and effort creating the presentation.

Answer the prompts below to determine if webinars are a tool you can use to launch your business.

What are the pros and cons to using a webinar to launch your business?

_____

_____

_____

What strategies will you use to get attendees for your webinar?

_____

_____

_____

What software will you use to host your webinar?

_____

_____

_____

What is the topic for your webinar?

_____

How will you present your webinar to attendees (PowerPoint, whiteboard, screen share, or other formats)?

_____

_____

_____

Podcast Interviews. Depending on the podcast, listenership numbers, and turnaround time from interview to airdate, podcast interviews are an option to launch your business.

Keep in mind, it is not enough to have one podcast interview. You need to have a series of interviews for this strategy to be effective in getting your business started.

There are tons of podcast hosts that are always looking for guests. So find a podcast that has your target audience as listeners (similar or complementary to your business, but not a direct competitor) and request an interview.

Based on your previous market research, identify 3 to 5 podcasts (that already have your target audience as listeners) to approach for an interview and write the names below.

_____

_____

_____

Podcast Advertising. Just like you can advertise on Google and your favorite social media platform, you can also advertise on podcasts as well. So grab the same podcaster list you used to generate a list for potential interviews to reach out to podcast hosts about their advertising opportunities. You can also reach out to me regarding advertising opportunities on my podcast Da Boss Experience Podcast (bit.ly/DaBossExperiencePodcast) if your target audience is female entrepreneurs.

Based on your previous market research, identify 3 to 5 podcasts that have your target audience as listeners and offer advertising opportunities. Write the names below.

_____

_____

_____

Blog Posts. Blogging is long-form written content that educates your target audience about a topic related to the problem you solve. While blogging is not an activity that will get you clients, right away, it can be an effective long-term marketing strategy. The reason some entrepreneurs find blogging effective is that it gives you the opportunity to show your target audience that you are an expert in your industry.

Probably the biggest benefit of blogging is something you do not hear a lot about and that is Search Engine Optimization (SEO). SEO allows your blog post and website to be discovered via Google. This is extremely important because Google can send you traffic if you optimize your blog post correctly.

So if you plan to Blog, use the same 3-4 core topic areas you identified in the social media section. Then write 30 Blog Post topics below.

_____

_____

_____

_____

_____

_____

_____

Guest Blog Post. Another way to get the word out about your business is guest blogging for someone that already has your target audience as readers or followers. When you guest blog, you get your blog post and information about your program, product, or service in front of a larger audience. This is a great way to promote your business because not only do bloggers post the blog on their website, but they notify their potentially sizable email list about the post as well. While guest blogging is a wonderful long-term marketing strategy, it may or may not be the best business launch approach. Answer the prompts below if you plan to use guest blogging in your long-term marketing plan.

Based on your previous market research, identify 3 to 5 blogs (that have your target audience as readers) to approach for a guest blogging partnership.

_____

_____

_____

Pinterest. Pinterest is a search engine with 444 million monthly active users worldwide. The platform operates as a search engine like Google. This means if you take the time to use the right keywords in your Pin titles and descriptions, you can get more traction and sales. An added bonus to using Pinterest is people can purchase what you sell directly from the platform.

Pinterest also has advertising available on the platform so you could potentially get an ad in front of your target audience pretty quickly. This makes Pinterest a great option as a short-term and long-term marketing strategy.

How do you envision using Pinterest for your business?

_____

_____

_____

What action will you take to learn more about using Pinterest for business? (Watch My Podcast Episode About Pinterest https://youtu.be/4EgekHnJ4Lg)

_____

_____

_____

Set A Launch Date

As much as you want to start your business immediately, give yourself time to properly launch your business. Once you complete all of the prompts outlined in the previous sections of this Business Launch Planner, you want to devote some time to just market and launch your new business. On the following page is a template for you to plot out your business launch details. Take your responses to the prompts in this section, and place the activity on the template.

Again, be very specific when you will...
- Send Your Marketing Emails (ex. friends and family, past customers, coworkers, neighbors, marketing list, network, etc...)
- Be Active On Social Media (Lives, Posts, Stories, DMs to Warm Relationships)
- Launch Your Influencer Marketing Ad
- Run Promotions (pricing, bundling, bonuses, product samples)
- Host Your Webinar
- Post On Pinterest
- Blog Posts
- Run Your Paid Ads (Facebook, Instagram, Influencers, YouTube)

*Be sure to reflect on the template how many times throughout the pre-launch period you will send emails, go Live, host a webinar, and so on.

**Do not feel compelled to use all of the marketing strategies mentioned in this business launch planner. Use the marketing activities that are best for your business, budget, and resources.

PRE-LAUNCH TEMPLATE
30 Days Before Business Launch

Month: _____

Week 1:

Monday _____

Tuesday _____

Wednesday _____

Thursday _____

Friday _____

Saturday _____

Sunday _____

Notes: _____

_____

_____

Week 2:

Monday _____

Tuesday _____

Wednesday _____

Thursday _____

Friday _____

Saturday _____

Sunday _____

Notes: _____

_____

_____

Week 3:

Monday _____

Tuesday _____

Wednesday _____

Thursday _____

Friday _____

Saturday _____

Sunday _____

Notes: _____

_____

_____

Week 4:

Monday _____

Tuesday _____

Wednesday _____

Thursday _____

Friday _____

Saturday _____

Sunday _____

Notes: _____

_____

_____

POST-LAUNCH TEMPLATE
30 Days After Business Launch

Month: _____

Week 1:

Monday _____

Tuesday _____

Wednesday _____

Thursday _____

Friday _____

Saturday _____

Sunday _____

Notes: _____

_____

_____

Week 2:

Monday _____

Tuesday _____

Wednesday _____

Thursday _____

Friday _____

Saturday _____

Sunday _____

Notes: _____

_____

_____

Week 3:

Monday _____

Tuesday _____

Wednesday _____

Thursday _____

Friday _____

Saturday _____

Sunday _____

Notes: _____

_____

_____

Week 4:

Monday _____

Tuesday _____

Wednesday _____

Thursday _____

Friday _____

Saturday _____

Sunday _____

Notes: _____

_____

_____

Step 5

Create Sustainable Business Systems

Establish Sustainable Business Systems

Incorporating standard operating procedures in your business means you have a written document that outlines how you operate. By taking the time to write down your systems and processes, you...

- Document how your business operates
- Identify what works in your business and change what does not
- Seamlessly onboard future freelancers and team members
- Efficiently train others to replicate your results
- Work on your business as a CEO instead of working in your business

As you move through this section to answer the prompts, it may feel strange thinking about the growth of your business before you make your first sale. However, establishing a foundation and a plan for business growth needs to happen in your business right from the start.

Defining the tasks in your business

This section provides an overview of some standard tasks associated with operating an online business. While you will wear many hats in the beginning stages of starting your business, you want to identify and systemize your daily tasks early on.

Review the tasks in this section to determine what is essential for your business. Then use the prompts to write out detailed procedures. Also, think about what tasks you can automate, outsource, and entrust to a team member as you move through this section.

Client Management and Support (ex. Client Service Records, Customer Service Questions, Check-Ins, Facebook Group Moderation, Client Terminations).

_____

_____

_____

Communication (ex. Team, External Partnerships, General Email Management).

_____

_____

_____

Copywriting (ex. Website, Product and/or Service Descriptions, Ads, Sales Email Series, Sales Page, and Other Written Content for Your Business).

_____

_____

_____

Client Onboarding (ex. Client Enrollment Meetings, Client Agreement Execution, Payment Processing, Payment Plan Approval).

_____

_____

_____

Marketing and Sales (ex. Lead Generation, Ad Creation, Media Opportunity Research, Sponsorship, Testimonial Collection, Customer Review Management, Product Promotions, Sales Calls, Order Fulfillment).

_____

_____

_____

Product Management (ex. Product Sourcing, Fulfillment Partners, Market Research, Product Development).

_____

_____

_____

Operations (ex. Team And Freelancer Management and Training, Project Management).

_____

_____

_____

Social Media Management (ex. Content Creation, Post Scheduling, Engagement, Comment Responses).

_____

_____

_____

Password Management and Protocol To Safeguard (ex. Social Media and Business Account Login Passwords).

_____

_____

_____

Account Access (ex. PayPal, Stripe, Square).

_____

_____

_____

Data Tracking and Management (ex. Sales, Key Performance Indicators, Expenses, Revenue Goals, Client Enrollment Goals).

_____

_____

_____

Refund Policy (ex. Money Back Guarantee, Chargebacks, Process for Return).

_____

_____

_____

Other Tasks.

_____

_____

_____

Each business is unique. Depending on the type of business you launch, you will undoubtedly incorporate specific processes into your standard operating procedures based on your operational needs. So use the information in this section and from the rest of this Business Launch Panner to develop what works best for your business.

Now let us review some Next Steps for your entrepreneurial journey.

Next Steps

Take The Next Step To Start Your Business

Starting a business is no easy task. You will invest time, money, heart, and soul into launching your business, so you want to get as many things right the first time around. Without mentorship to guide you through the business launch process, you can feel overwhelmed trying to figure everything out on your own. That is why this Business Launch Planner is the perfect resource to get you started with your business.

As you can imagine, I cannot teach you everything you need to know about starting a business. In this section, I want to share with you how you can work with me as a student of my CEO Boss Academy (**bit.ly/34K5TNp**).

CEO Blueprint Academy (**bit.ly/34K5TNp**) is a 90-day group coaching program to help you refine everything you learned in this planner. I hold your hand as we move through the following 5-Step Blueprint to Start Your Business:

Step 1 - Foundation. I share a simple process to help you discover expertise and experiences you probably forgot about or are ignoring because you do not believe you can create a business from it. We also dive into goal setting and confront any issues that may become barriers to your success.

Step 2 - Package Your Offer. I give you a strategy to take all of the passion, skills, knowledge, expertise, and experiences you discovered in Step 1 to refine your business idea.

Step 3 - Create Your Business Plan. I show you how to vet your business idea for profitability and how to develop your business plan.

Step 4 - Launch Your Business. I walk you through developing a marketing strategy to launch your business so you can steadily get clients.

Step 5 - Create Sustainable Business Systems. I guide you on how to implement systems in your business to outsource, hire teams, and create a real company that allows you to develop and grow your business as a CEO.

In addition to everything I just mentioned, I also have the following

BONUSES for you:

Bonus 1: Business Resource Toolkit
With so many different software programs, it can be confusing trying to figure out which tools meet your business needs. I made it easy for you by compiling this Business Resource Toolkit to help you identify which tools you need for every stage and aspect of your business.

Bonus 2: Client Management Forms
Take the guesswork out of figuring out which forms you need to create for your business with my client management template pack. These forms help you screen, onboard, and manage client issues. All you have to do is tweak the forms to fit your business needs.

Bonus 3: Operational Manual Template
The key to creating a business that operates without you is systems. Having systems in your business helps to lay the foundation for creating processes that enable you, a member of your team, or even a family member to replicate every aspect of your business including your results. When you enroll in CEO Blueprint Academy (**bit.ly/34K5TNp**), you get a business systems template that you can modify to fit your business.

Bonus 4: Personalized Business Strategy Call

I provide 1 personalized coaching strategy session during the 90-day program. This 90-minute Zoom session is designed to provide you individualized support launching your specific business.

Bonus 5: Weekly Q&A Sessions

Q&A Sessions are held weekly via my private Facebook Group. These sessions either center around one topic or provide Q&A.

Book A Call With Me To Apply - I Only Enroll A Limited Number Of People, So Apply Today

https://bit.ly/CEOBlueprintAcademy

www.ingramcontent.com/pod-product-compliance
Lightning Source LLC
Chambersburg PA
CBHW080611220526
45466CB00010B/3313